THE NATIONAL POETRY SERIES

The National Poetry Series was established in 1978 to ensure the publication of five poetry books annually through five participating publishers. Publication is funded by the Lannan Foundation; Stephen Graham; Joyce & Seward Johnson Foundation; Glenn and Renee Schaeffer, Juliet Lea Hillman Simonds Foundation; Tiny Tiger Foundation; and Charles B. Wright III.

2007 COMPETITION WINNERS

Joe Bonomo of DeKalb, Illinois, *Installations*
Chosen by Naomi Shihab Nye, Penguin Books

Oni Buchanan of Brighton, Massachusetts, *Spring*
Chosen by Mark Doty, University of Illinois Press

Sabra Loomis of New York, New York, *House Held Together by Winds*
Chosen by James Tate, HarperCollins Publishers

Donna Stonecipher of Berlin, Germany, *The Cosmopolitan*
Chosen by John Yau, Coffee House Press

Rodrigo Toscano of Brooklyn, New York, *Collapsible Poetics Theater*
Chosen by Marjorie Welish, Fence Books

The Cosmopolitan

POEMS

Donna Stonecipher

Coffee House Press
MINNEAPOLIS
2008

COVER & BOOK DESIGN Coffee House Press

Cover collage by Jiří Kolář (1914–2002).
Thanks to Běla Kolářová and the Helcls for permission.
Thanks also to Jana Pelouchová of Museum Kampa.
Special thanks to Aleksandar Manić for his help
in securing the rights.

Coffee House Press books are available to the trade through our primary distributor, Consortium Book Sales & Distribution, 1045 Westgate Drive, Saint Paul, MN 55114. For personal orders, catalogs, or other information, write to: Coffee House Press, 27 North Fourth Street, Suite 400, Minneapolis, MN 55401.

Coffee House Press is a nonprofit literary publishing house. Support from private foundations, corporate giving programs, government programs, and generous individuals helps make the publication of our books possible. We gratefully acknowledge their support in detail in the back of this book.

Good books are brewing at coffeehousepress.org

LIBRARY OF CONGRESS CATALOGING-IN-PUBLICATION DATA
Stonecipher, Donna
The cosmopolitan : poems / by Donna Stonecipher.
p. cm.
ISBN 978-1-56689-221-6 (alk. paper)
I. Title.
PS3619.T685C67 2008
811'.6—DC22
2008012527

FIRST EDITION | FIRST PRINTING
1 3 5 7 9 8 6 4 2

PRINTED IN THE UNITED STATES

Notes and Acknowledgments

In "Inlay 18 (Sei Shonagan)," the image of a cuckoo clock broadcasting the call of the muezzin is based on an artwork by Via Lewandowsky. In "Inlay 11 (Zaha Hadid)," the "Self-Portrait of the King's Portraitist" is a photograph by Robert Polidori. In "Inlay 9 (Azar Nafisi)," reference is made to this quote by the architect Dominique Perrault: "It is 'time' itself that is undoubtedly the object of the architect's whole attention, his only preoccupation, the permanent restlessness of a present he tirelessly seeks to actualize." I found this displayed in Otto Wagner's Postsparkasse in Vienna.

Many thanks to the editors of the journals in which some of these poems first appeared: *New American Writing*, *Denver Quarterly*, *The Canary*, *Coconut*, *GutCult*, *Upstairs at Duroc*, *Absent Magazine*, *Europe* (France), *Po&sie* (France). "Inlay 1 (Franz Kafka)" was printed as a broadside for The Floating Edition, Berlin, Germany. Thanks to Jesse Seldess and Leonie Weber. "Inlay 21 (Ralph Waldo Emerson)" was written for the project "Lettre : L'Autre" in Paris in October 2006. Thank you to Sarah Riggs and Omar Berrada. Special thanks to Josepha Conrad, Millay Hyatt, and Veronika Reichl. Extra-special thanks and much more to Emmanuel Moses, whose boundless faith in these poems sustained the writing of them. And finally, my gratitude to John Yau.

For L.C.

Contents

Note to the Reader

These poems were written while I was thinking about my generation's relationship to quotation and collage. After a visit to the Metropolitan Museum's furniture collection, during which I looked at the inlaid furniture, followed by an encounter in another museum with one of Joseph Cornell's boxes, in which a postcard was hung by a pin, the first Inlay was born. As with these relationships, the inlaid quotes here are (mostly) autonomous within the surrounding poems; the quotes are from books I happened to be reading during the period the poems were written, when I was living in Berlin.

Inlay 1 (Franz Kafka)

1.

If the beekeeper didn't steal it, what would the honeybees do with their honey? the little girl asked her mother, who was placing her nose in a tiger lily's interior spotted with the suggestion of disease. Meanwhile the spade-shaped red leaves were coming off all too easily in the brother's upstretched hand.

2.

In the darkening twilight, he sat reading a novel in which someone was reading a novel in which someone was reading a novel in which someone was reading a novel in which a miniature woman was turning the pages of a miniature novel wearing a miniature thimble. Blue-edged clouds (floating world)

3.

The architect was internationally famous before she'd ever built a single building. She traveled the world giving lectures to well-bespectacled crowds. The bridge is reflected gently in the river, its gesture kindly reversed. Half the apartment building's windows shone gold in the evening's nightly revolution.

4.

Trying to remember her dream in the plane was like trying to sieve water from water. It was like trying to look at one's eyes with one's own eyes, without the aid of the mirror's galactic eye. She thought the life vest far too complicated, and sat back and closed her eyes. The dream had been full of schadenfreude.

5.

This thought, of a woman wearing a thimble, made him sexually crazy. He was flipping through a book of French daguerreotypes when the blue velvet encasing the picture of two long-gone *filles de joie* made him think of the sky at dusk when his mother would call him in for dinner in an American suburb long ago.

6.

He didn't want his girlfriend in a locket. He didn't want his wife on her knees tweeting like a canary in a cage. He didn't want a frame around a face freezing his beloved into a smiling simulacrum, her eyes simulacra of eyes that had watched him coming toward her through the darkness on that authentic night.

7.

The theoretical buildings gave off a certain rarefied beauty. The architect lived in an apartment on the fifth floor. Her theories were crystallizing nicely in their books, and her drawings were of buildings that like butterflies made of glass could never live. Who would tether a castle in Spain to Spain?

"The little wooden stairway did not reveal anything,
no matter how long one regarded it"

8.

Her restlessness was mounting. She wanted to transform herself into a taut construction composed of thread and ballasts at maximal tilt. And when at last she was as tense as possible, her physical being would slip like a glob of honey through the knots and dissolve into the fracas masquerading as "the world."

9.

He flipped and flipped through the book of French daguerreotypes. Naked girls; dead infants; views of Paris; famous writers; Indians; families all in blue. He stopped at a picture of a naked girl kissing a bewildered Persian kitten. He stopped at a picture of a dead infant drowned in a deluge of white frills.

10.

If the beekeeper didn't steal it, what *would* the honeybees do with their honey? the father wondered. After the party she thought, if there's one thing I need to do in this life, it's work on my poker face. A woman in a blue coat knocked at the door. When she took off her mohair gloves, he could see she was wearing a thimble.

Inlay 2 (Elaine Scarry)

1.

If only our troubles were those of the architect. In which the solution is born at the same time as the problem. The architect has simply to work her way toward it, through a dark tunnel or a prescribed maze. Which proves the marvelous fact that there are cases in life where ingenuity is not the primary virtue — but rather tenacity.

2.

You keep doing it, he said to her one night. You keep moving across town and then feeling the "lost" streets pulling you back like a siren song, all disfigured by hope. This time let it be the swan song. Let the dying swan glide through your canals and then sink to the bottom like a piece of Cleopatra's dysfunctional bâteau.

3.

You can know the aristocratic pretensions of a scene by the proportion of sky to landscape, she ruminated in the museum. The more sky, the more elegant the tiny Russians strolling along the embankment twirling parasols. If a sky can be profligate, what limit the bankrolls nestled in fustian pockets?

4.

Which would you rather your head be full of, facts or ideas? (Clouds, riposted the cosmopolitan.) Facts are finite, said the dreamer. Ideas reproduce exponentially, said the monkey. But inside every fact is an idea, said the beautiful girl. But inside every idea is a beautiful girl, said the man in a brown study.

5.

The voluntary exile dreamed of the clouds that form over her native city. There she knew the names of all the birds. She had learned this voluntarily, by application. But all kinds of knowledge collects like sediment in local minds, useless but for ballast — which, as all exiles know, should never be underestimated.

6.

If only our troubles were those of the town planner. On our freshly prepared grid, where to position the park, the town hall, the elementary school, the bored housewife fucking the plumber? The town is a given. The town waits like a fate for the town planner, who slowly reveals it with a blue pencil.

"Daydreaming originates in the volitional"

7.

"Ideally, I'd look like a Spaniard, fuck like a Serb, and make money hand over fist like an American," said the cosmopolitan sitting in Hong Kong drinking a caipirinha. Only the American bristled. *The reflective man, the genius, the seer, the torchbearer, the radical, the spiritualist, the moral high-hogger*

8.

She had climbed all the stairs of pleasure and was shocked to find no issue at the top. So pleasure has a glass ceiling: or, the idea of more pleasure can form in the mind, but the fact of more pleasure in the body cannot. The girl lying next to her bed could not stop putting her hand into the bag of little candy hearts.

9.

The citizen has ideas about the architect, but the architect has ideas about the citizen. The architect needs the citizens to people the plaza. But do the citizens need the architect? Yes, for the architect tells the citizens precisely how far they are willing to trust modernity — and precisely how far they are not.

10.

If only our troubles were those of the bellboy. In which the world shrinks to a glowing pageant of installation and abandonment. The problem of the polished permanence of the temporary. And the vicarious thrill of holding all that has come under another's sphere of influence in one's own gloved hands.

11.

For years, she admitted one night, my fantasy was this: buying a house, arranging it with my things, shopping for sofas and hassocks, and then locking it up and renting an apartment in a neighboring city. In the apartment I would always have flowers on my kitchen table: dahlias in September, and peonies in late spring.

12.

Facts are finite, but ideas feed on facts to achieve infinity. The architect sat down to his plans. The voluntary exile never learned the names of the birds in her adopted city. Each bird was a foreigner, flitting through the trees and singing a beautiful mysterious song she hadn't the remotest desire to comprehend.

Inlay 3 (Jonathan Raban)

1.

She was learning that desire, most prodigal gift, bore a little price tag, so small you needed a magnifying glass to see it. She didn't want to look the tiniest gift horse in the mouth. The horse was galloping away, probably to Zermatt, a blue dot on the map. She sat in the café, twisting her ring and ruing her equanimity.

2.

Each day they walked past a door with a tarnished brass plaque that read Institut freudien de Psychanalyse, and one day he gestured meaningfully toward it and said, "It's always closed." It didn't matter, there was plenty of hot sunshine that empty August, and they fucked a lot. The bakeries were always about half full.

3.

The Tintorettos are in Vienna, and the Vermeers are in New York. The Hoppers are in Paris, and the Gainsboroughs are in L.A. The da Vinci is under lock and key in a house on the outskirts of Seattle. The author took the elevator up to the special collections at the library, to whom she'd (prematurely, she now realized) sold her papers.

4.

At the dinner party, there was a pair of Rilke's letters framed on the bookshelf. In the first, said our hostess, he was coaxing his mistress to meet him in Vienna. The second, written a week later, was a hasty apology; he was sorry, Vienna wasn't going to work out. We marveled at the beauty of the capital letters, and then dessert was served.

5.

I want to spend an entire day reclining on the balcony eating nothing but dark chocolate. We walked under the awnings of fancy hotels and were reminded that life could be otherwise, but when we walked past the poor we felt on the contrary reinforced in our own destinies, we felt our skins tightening over our justifiable collection of bones.

"There's no history in a wilderness. It just *is*."

6.

London has its Rothko, and Paris has its Rothko. New York has its Rothko, and Des Moines has its Rothko. Tokyo has its Rothko, and Berlin has its Rothko. Venice has its Rothko, and Geneva has its Rothko. After walking among imperial fountains she felt that if she opened her own mouth a jet of water would suddenly come spurting out.

7.

We just happened upon the amusement park. We gave in to the concertina. Up high on the Ferris wheel we looked down and sweetly remembered. The wife called the husband in the middle of the night as he lay with his new girlfriend and said if he didn't come to collect his books by the morning, she'd throw them out the window onto the street.

8.

She liked Art Nouveau at different phases in her life. At nineteen she felt a delightful shock of recognition at the curves. At twenty-six she was disgusted by all things vegetal. At thirty-four she suspected the whole thing of bad taste, and at forty-five she fell in love with a picture of a building by Guimard, as though it were a picture of her in her youth.

9.

And the nosegay of violets in the detail of the Manet on the cover of the copy of Baudelaire? No one can say exactly why all it takes is a nightlight to nourish les fleurs du mal. *Souviens-toi que le Temps est un joueur avide.* You sat on the made bed surrounded by a disheveled mess of half-read books and felt that yes, it might be possible to die happy.

Inlay 4 (Susan Sontag)

1.

If you've been to a city's airport, can you say you have been to that city? Things tended to happen of a Sunday, more than of a Tuesday or a Saturday. It was like being in a silent film, where we spoke to each other with great emotion, but no words at all were coming out of our mouths.

2.

She hung up the world map on her wall and considered the conquerable entity. Next to it, she placed colored pushpins in a box. Everyone complained that border officials no longer stamped passports, but her great sorrow was that it was impossible to get hotels to put stickers on her portmanteau.

3.

The girl with the titian hair wearing a botticelli pink delacroix jacket was said to have rubenesque curves. We were mourning privately the decline of the extraction industries as we glanced out of the train window at the harbor: this "natural" landscape feature clearly meant to be used.

4.

The first thing he would do upon entering any hotel room was to open all the drawers in the desks and bureaus. A Bible, a volume of poems, a shoehorn — he knew that one day *it* would be there. The encyclopedists would have laughed — they knew how to finesse something out of nothing.

5.

She turned her profile toward the Occident. He turned his profile toward the Orient. As they bent to examine lilies in the museum garden she said to him, I'd give all the photographs ever taken of me for a single painted portrait. In a gold frame. Idealized, of course. Ideally even allegorized.

"the inauthenticity of the beautiful"

6.

More and more, the image of contentment in my head was of Saint Jerome in his study. I collected postcards of all the renditions of him absorbed in his books, and propped them up on my own books. Wasn't this then happiness — to be contained within life like a big mind inside a bigger mind?

7.

How many stacked-up peacock feathers does it take for the feeling of weightlessness to be overestimated? She kept one peacock feather in a drawer. We knew they were dynamiting mountaintops in West Virginia, but still we were two flâneurs in the city, pointing out things we liked in shop windows.

8.

I opened my mouth and out flew the butterfly from China. You opened your mouth and out flew the canary from the coalmine. *This place is Kafkaesque*, he grumbled to himself in line at the bank in the strange city, waiting for a lamp with the right number finally to light up. *Even if it is Prague.*

9.

Free at last to roam where she liked in the museum, she found herself heliotropically drawn to the portraits in profile. The whole face told too much; the Venetian girl gazing fixedly to the left kept a seemingly effortless hold on her mystery. And the pink buildings enforced their symmetry.

10.

If airports counted, she could more than double her list of vanquished cities. And if train stations counted? Her eyes lit up. She was not now, nor would she ever be, the girl in the port. (A shipful of drunken sailors was just an invitation to her to spill raspberry juice on somebody's white pants.)

II.

It was like being in a silent film — we had to wait for the intertitles, which took forever to translate a little of the profusion in our heads into phrases. Pity we who must corset our mental splendor into the whalebone of grammar, which laces us up so tight we have to remove a rib to breathe.

Inlay 5 (Erwin Panofsky)

1.

We lay on the grass in the botanical garden dreaming that the whole world was a botanical garden, with little white plastic tags labeling every object visible or invisible to the eye. Every little purple geodesic dome and violet-blue vortex. Every outwhorling leaf and inwhorling umbel.

2.

He turned off the light in his kitchen and all that remained of the cat were its two sacral eyes. They floated somewhere above the chair. Don't blink, little egyptian, he thought, and plunge me into a darkness more dark than the darkness I know lies at the back of your black hole of a heart.

3.

There would be white tags labeling corollas with snow-white pistils, and labeling deep green fronds. There would be tags labeling trees with leaves shaped like the tree itself and trees with no leaves left. There would be tags labeling a true genus and a false genus, and that's where we'd lie down.

4.

She wondered how many people secretly hoped, as she did, that "progress" would in the nick of time be stopped, that the past with its wasting diseases and victrolas would suddenly resurface like a reflection in a pool troubled by some reckless interruption. He gave her a recycled dragonfly.

5.

The etymology of venereal disease is Venus, he was stunned to read in his dictionary. Not venal. Meanwhile, the people standing in the field were waiting for the UFO they knew would one day come with a confused love in their hearts, a love that could move mountains, that could befog time.

6.

A racehorse cannot be given the name of any other racehorse that ever raced. So Affirmed and Cigar race only into the past, like horses in a painting hanging in a hotel. In a name there hides a destiny — like a Chinese cookie, or a Fabergé egg — a history pneumatically smashed into the hereafter.

"Man is indeed the only animal to leave records behind him,
for he is the only animal whose products 'recall to mind'
an idea distinct from their material existence"

7.

The cosmopolitan knows the difference between the Hutus and the Tutsis. The former citadel is used today exclusively for cultural purposes. The former brewery is used today exclusively for cultural purposes. The former porcelain factory is used today exclusively for cultural purposes.

8.

There would be a tag labeling the pale-pink bract and a tag labeling the tree with the diseased white trunk. We would know for certain what was Myanmar and what was Burma, what was Mumbai and what was Bombay. We would know clementines from tangerines, sincerity from flattery.

9.

O vatic, lowly votive of the caption. He bought a book of oval cyanotypes of the early Mississippi River and stared night after night at the blue irrigation ditches, the blue steamboats and blue bluffs. It wasn't long before his dreams of having sex with his ex-girlfriend were all tinted blue.

10.

But the peacock island still reigns: and here idolatry cannot be said to be mere. We reached it by broken-down ferryboat, we looked at the world spangled black and green and blue, we plunged into the voluptuousness of feathers that do not fly. We have never been to the peacock island.

II.

There were white tags labeling the fern that looked like a citadel and the flower whose open mouth was stuffed with tiny croziers. We lay on the grass in the botanical garden among thousands of white tags and daydreamed that there were no more mysteries of nomenclature left in this world.

Inlay 6 (Mary B. Campbell)

1.

She sat down to build her day like a townhouse: room stacked atop room filled with pretexts for activity to save herself from falling headlong into undifferentiated time. If we could architecturalize time, we could make ourselves a home in it. Her calendar was a citadel of square rooms, her agenda a high-rise of many storeys.

2.

On that extravagant Saturday afternoon, the xenophile met the xenophobe as planned in front of the giraffes. But when they kissed, one dissolved and one accrued. Not for all the tea in China, not for all the gold in Russia would the small country alter its history books to accommodate the delusions of the big country.

3.

The group of students touring Chartres was told by the bespectacled guide that the stained-glass pictures were not merely pretty, but actually scripture for the illiterate. Years later one of the students would remember this while reading at a desk facing a window and think: What beauty isn't born out of the missionary position?

4.

There are things that cannot be taught, that can only be learned. She wondered why in Renaissance paintings, the landscapes tiered out into the distance are rendered entirely in degrees of blue. Voltaire said, "a practically infallible way of preserving yourself against self-destruction is always to have something to do."

5.

Standing in front of the three Raphael madonnas in the museum, the man wrote in his notebook: *Read the pre-Raphaelite manifesto. If they wrote one.* Meanwhile, in the next room, a woman was looking at Saint Catherine and thinking: I prefer the symbolic to the allegorical. I prefer the iconographic to the realistic.

6.

Does every small town here have a disused castle? Does every small-town disused castle here have a park? Does every small-town disused castle park here have a maze? Does every small-town disused castle park maze here have an issue onto a formal garden where white violets flower in the form of a fleur-de-lys?

"All painting is, in a way, still life"

7.

A swan was menacing the rowboat they had rented to take a spin around the small artificial lake stocked with swans. She remembered reading that with a single blow of its heavenly white wings a swan could kill a man if it so chose. Her lover reclined awkwardly in the stern staring up at the fluffy white clouds.

8.

O things that cannot be taught. The bluer the day, the more it infuses itself with the blue of the sky, and with the blue of the lake infusing itself with the blue of the sky, which then offers its infused blue scrupulously back. The distant sky blue landscape was set like the painter's inner ideal landscape into the painting.

9.

"Tomorrow" may be space, but "today" is time, time drowning in its own moat, time watching its own dimensions float, deflate from a castle down to a vestibule. In the Paris of the Prairies they were dreaming of the Paris of the Middle East. In the Venice of the North they were dreaming of the Venice of the West.

10.

The cosmopolitan looked in the mirror, raised an eyebrow, and said: *A man, a plan, a canal, Panama.* The symbol is purer, the woman wrote in her notebook, than the allegory, because the distance between the symbol and the symbolized is neatly collapsed by time. She drew a pomegranate, and then an oriole.

11.

The figure holding a miniature stone castle could only be Saint Barbara. The figure encircled by entranced birds could only be Saint Francis. The man cursed softly to himself. It was so hard to keep it straight — Lucas Cranach *the Younger*, but Hans Holbein *the Elder*. Which would you rather have, money or innocence?

12.

She laid aside her pens, agendas, and calendars, lit another cigarette, and opened up the day's *International Herald-Tribune*, where she read: "The Mona Lisa was last loaned out (to Tokyo and Moscow) in 1974. It will never again be loaned out, say museum officials. For the foreseeable future, it has a permanent home."

13.

That's what she wanted, like the Mona Lisa: a permanent home. The second hand was marching efficiently around the clock's face, in one perfected mechanism consuming and ridding itself of time. At midnight, high up in the astrological clock tower, a door opened and out came a little grinning skeleton ringing a black bell.

14.

To move through the day like a pilgrim achieving each station of the cross. To wait on the French balcony for the lover or for the menacing swan. To wander through the small-town disused castle's unkempt maze, glad for the imposition of a route. To reflect on the stained-glass windows at Chartres: dogma aided by light.

Inlay 7 (Franz Kafka)

1.

He travelled to Japan but he didn't see any geishas. He travelled to Kenya but he didn't see any giraffes. When he opened the book, he was surprised to find inside it another book. After a bad night in room 536, the hotel pool swallowed him like a square blue mouth swallowing a sleeping pill.

2.

It is hard to rip up a photograph with a face in it. In the tiniest torn-up piece, the face is still intact. The face lies smiling up from the bottom of the wastebasket, and then smiles as it falls out of the garbage truck onto a lawn, and then smiles as it drifts slowly across the city back to your door.

3.

Young people from the less powerful country came over to study the language of the more powerful neighboring country. The questionnaire found that, within a small margin of error, such-and-such percentage of women prefer to be on their knees while performing such-and-such sexual acts.

4.

She felt like crying when she read in the paper that déjà vu was a chemical reaction in the body and not a magical window into existences previous and future at all. The oval mirror hanging by a black ribbon above the mantel reflected part of the dark sofa and the smile on the porcelain geisha lamp.

5.

The Russian exile with blue eyes admitted — not without a certain pride — that he had an accent in every language: A Russian accent speaking German, a German accent speaking Russian, an indeterminate accent speaking English, and an English accent when speaking indeterminately.

6.

The language liquefaction. Sexy attempts at traction. A smattering of satisfaction. He held the word up to the light like a spectacularly faceted chit. She wondered if it were true what she had read, that when one speaks a foreign language, one cannot help but become a member of that foreign tribe.

> "What you say sounds reasonable enough," said the man, "but I refuse to be bribed. I am here to whip people, and whip them I shall."

7.

The silent majority stared hard at the vocal minority. More and more, there were eyes closing as velvet curtains descended upon screens. More and more, there were hands turning on electric lights in the daytime. More and more, there were cosmopolitans carefully examining tropical flowers in the dark.

8.

The young people from the less powerful country did not stop to admire the complicated beauty of their new language's intricate grammar. They made neat vocabulary lists in cheap notebooks, and in their own language made fun of the professor's hair, accent, glasses, clothing, shoes, and laugh.

9.

In Paris the American girl speaking French began almost imperceptibly to bat her eyelashes. In St. Paul the German boy speaking English had the urge to fill silences almost before they began. One of the most marvelous memories of her life, she said, was of having déjà vu of having had déjà vu.

10.

He travelled to France but he didn't see any existentialists. He travelled to Italy but he didn't see dolce far niente. He travelled to China but he didn't see any panda bears. He travelled to California but he didn't see a single surfer. Nevertheless his shell collection, with every vacation, grew.

Inlay 8 (Claude Lévi-Strauss)

1.

He was born in Kaya, Burkina Faso, but now he's living abroad. She was born in Frankfurt, Germany, but now she's living abroad. She was born in Seoul, South Korea, but now she's living abroad. He was born in Vancouver, Washington, but now he's living abroad.

2.

And if she ran the city through a sieve, as she sometimes imagined doing, would she be left with only the natives, pedigreed and pure? Everybody, eventually, goes down the Philosophenweg, gaping at hieroglyphic heirloom roses and beetles with supersvelte legs.

3.

He's like me, he said. He has an inner map of hotels all over Europe. And it was true: if we met a man from Cologne, he'd get a faraway look in his eyes and eventually work the conversation around to say, ". . . and tell me, do you know the marvelous Hotel Dom?"

4.

As for me, I would choose to infiltrate foreign territories via the spice route rather than the silk route. Nutmeg, mint, cinnamon, aniseed, turmeric, cardamom, the hotel, the parliament. I sat in the reproduction victoria thinking about the myth of the bequeathal of the family house.

"I hate traveling and explorers."

5.

She was born in Montpellier, France, but now she's living in London. He was born in Miramar, Argentina, but now he's living in Tokyo. He was born on an island in the Caribbean, but now he's living in Paris. She was born in Bangalore, India, but now she's living in L.A.

6.

"Bloom where you are planted," read the inspirational poster tacked up in her childhood classroom. She remembered the school's aquarium glowing dimly in the main hallway, and how the fish fulfilled some edifying dictum she could never, tiptoeing by, definitively figure out.

7.

But she had long since shed that skin, and that skin had long since shed her: the school no longer existed, except as an album of crumbling images in a small number of non-commemorative minds. Oh, there'd been so many worms — back when one was an early bird.

8.

The Pizzeria Inez became the Curry House Inez became the Sushi Inez, and all the while Parisians hurried past on their way to cafés recently overtaken by Chinese immigrants. Everyone goes down the Passage d'Enfer eventually, hushed by the shuttered windows and doors.

9.

From this airport alone, you could fly to Geneva, Fez, Malta, Alicante, Berlin, San Francisco, and Luxor. We'll do that one day, he said. We'll arrive at the airport with one suitcase each and fly to the destination that seems to us to hold the greatest promise of annihilation.

Inlay 9 (Azar Nafisi)

1.

She passed a store full of blue, yellow, and red messenger bags printed with the letters DDR. It was 2006, and she saw a girl inside the store lay her hand on a bag abstractedly, as if imagining herself here and there wearing the bag announcing the name of a country that no longer exists.

2.

The trees had begun their yearly unburdening. If only all of the stone houses were covered in ivy slowly dying into thousands of little red hands. I would like to lose my leaves like a tree he thought, walking in the shamelessly lush cemetery. Yes, I would like to unleaf like a tree.

3.

And down and down the Puschkinallee, and down and down the Prenzlauerallee. Was it true that the architect's only real object of attention was time? So even a house holds a paradox. Of the windows in the dusk, one couldn't say if the light was coming from without or from within.

4.

The hungover tourist happily bought the red T-shirt printed with the letters CCCP, though he couldn't say for sure what the letters stood for. She told us with a little frown that she had grown up on the Stalinallee, and then the Karl-Marx-Allee, and then again the Stalinallee (in her mind).

5.

Street names are a reliable guide to all that a city holds dear. So in the town of Elm, Oak, and Cherry streets we felt that the city's true history could be read only in the rings of the trees. The historian had a rage for order. One single paper out of place in her office and she couldn't work at all.

"It is said that the personal is political. That is not true, of course."

6.

Just when children and the elderly were going to bed, the rest of us were beginning to realize with a chill that sleep was, in fact, quite impossible. There was something called life, and it refused to stay unlived. In the window of the art-supply store crowded too many posable wooden hands.

7.

As the architect builds in space and thinks about time, so the clock on the mantel insists on ticking into a room that owes its rose-papered walls to the clock's disciplined existence. Quarter notes float motionless over the piano. The window opens like a thought onto the golden-yellow gingko.

8.

That night the girl with the DDR bag met the boy with the CCCP T-shirt in a bar. History does not record what followed — the fatal attraction, the hero worship, the erection of monuments, the pacts and the breaking of pacts, the inevitable bitter dissolution once again into sovereign states.

9.

She tried to think: How many years had it been since she'd lain tiny in her bed at night wearing huge headphones, believing every single ontological promise proffered by the notes of what was, after all, only a song? Lights, action, grammar, I mean camera, I mean glamour, I mean gla-di-o-la.

10.

Outside, in the People's Park, a flurry of yellow leaves like slow-motion feathers were in the midst of making their brief annual migration from marked branches to hard ground. In every Potemkin village there can be found a Potemkin, of that at least the rest of us can be reasonably sure.

11.

How marvelous, they thought, that it was possible to have been born in Chemnitz, spend your life in Karl-Marx-Stadt, and then die in Chemnitz, all without ever leaving your hometown. How marvelous to have been born in a country that no longer exists — though you do, you still exist.

Inlay 10 (Ralph Waldo Emerson)

1.

The old musical theater had been turned into a parking garage, but nobody had bothered to remove the ornaments, the gilding, the chandeliers. He parked his green Subaru across from the dark red velvet loges, put the car keys in his pocket, and got out.

2.

The city was turning into a memorial city, with memorials remembering the dead built into the living city like crumblings of original stone in a rebuilt stone cupola, dark squares randomly counterpointing the mass of new light squares, forming the sphere.

3.

She saved a white flower from Goethe's garden in her notebook. She had just seen the first box building built by the Bauhaus, and she knew that the white flower had been built, too, and furthermore by whom. An origami swan stood on the mantel.

4.

Every time a new store opened in the town shopping mall down the road, we all swore we couldn't remember what store had been in that spot before it. But why even try to hide your sadness behind a peacock-feather fan? Say, *Able was I ere I saw Elba.*

5.

Through his window, he saw the word CIGARETTES in art deco letters left above the lintel of the renovated building across the street. Having sex with his wife for the last time, he thought: So the past is invited into the future only in the form of signs.

6.

Like an empire without an emperor, like a park without a crystal palace, like a still life without a disingenuous dark insect set speculatively upon the lemon. She stood in front of the lit-up opera house and asked herself: Is a building dead or alive?

"The end of the human race will be that it will eventually
die of civilization"

7.

Memorials began moving into more and more of the area presumably meant for the living. The city was slowly turning into a city of the past. Though all cities have turned into cities of the past. As soon as a building is inhabited, it is dismantled by memory.

8.

The memorial's aim is to sap time. The memorial dreams of vanquished space. The memorial pretends innocence. The memorial is an artificial scar. The memorial wants to live forever. But the memorial is mortal. The memorial is amoral.

9.

The sightseeing boat floated slowly under the bridge, all of its green plastic chairs unoccupied. Each bridge was neatly engraved with the date of its completion, as though the act of collapsing space had to be fixed at a specific place in time.

10.

For the day is palindromic. The daytime reads into the nighttime, which reads backwards into the daytime. She thought that the garden, too, was palindromic, an array of white flowers reading into decay reading back into an array of white flowers come spring.

11.

White flower. Artificial scar. CIGARETTES. Like a park without a crystal palace, without a white flower built like a cupola, without an origami swan without its empire, built like a white flower. CIGARETTES. The green Subaru floated very slowly under the bridge.

12.

A timeline of bridges overwhelming liquidity. On their way to dinner at the Indian restaurant, they stopped before a memorial. Here something happened, the memorial said, that reads in only one direction. Something someone can't bear you to forget.

Inlay II (Zaha Hadid)

I.

Who needs leaves when there are so many white lights to string on the trees? The sleight of hand of winter recognizes the chicanery of the age of electricity. The snow announces its ingenuity with all the sangfroid of a cloud machine. The photographs of staircases gestured to ingress and egress, while denying us, the viewers, either one.

2.

Just because your last name is "King" doesn't mean you descend from royalty. The formal garden was a fitting antidote to the disarray growing wild in her mind. Wasn't symmetry a "natural" phenomenon, as natural as a replica, as a graph? He had always thought we'd be happier like snails, coiled up tightly inside spiral shells.

3.

After all, utopia *means* noplace. Of course the new office towers were *gleaming*. *Naturally* the view from the rooftop garden was *spectacular*. After the TV show, the young girl wanted to wear her hair in braids like a Chinese communist and shout slogans in the street; but the bicycles, one by one, were all going the way of the horse.

4.

But we knew nothing about it, sitting a world away at our sidewalk café. Funny, you remarked, how a small country doesn't feel small when you're in it. Drags of vastness are always at hand for those who know how to grasp them. Afterwards we headed off to the exhibit of trompe l'oeil paintings, but somehow we never were able to find it.

5.

"There will always be a certain segment of the population," said the erstwhile social worker, "that is poor." "Just as there will always be a certain segment of the population," said the cosmopolitan fingering a pearl earring, "that is chic." Oh we were sick to death of chic, overseen by laws that no one can identify but the chic themselves.

"Architecture is really about well-being"

6.

He liked to wander through big glamorous cities and feel excluded, up and down staircases at dusk as intimations of belonging were lit up window by window. He understood the relation between exclusionary and inclusionary zones in every individual's life, and how a delicate balance of each keeps one proportionately human.

7.

Blue pencil poised, she kept forgetting that there are no right angles in nature. The city council voted at last to rebuild the castle, vanished for fifty years, but upon closer questioning acquiesced that there'd be no need to build inside the façade, since there was no need to rebuild queen's quarters for queens that, after all, don't exist.

8.

Ah, but who doesn't tremble before the majesty of a real façade? At the factory of fake Wedgwoods we brooded on the fur of facsimile as we filled up our plastic baskets with powder-blue-and-white teapots and bowls. She was a great adherent of democracy, she said, but that didn't mean she didn't harbor secret totalitarian thoughts.

9.

We looked at the photograph called "Self-Portrait of the King's Portraitist." Right where the portraitist's face should have been was your face in the glass. I wouldn't say it was *exactly* like finding money in the pocket of a coat you haven't worn since last winter, but it was *a little* like the universe's seeming gift of something that was yours all along.

Inlay 12 (Owen Jones)

1.

She said, Why are there so many things I do know and wish I didn't, and so many things I don't know and wish I did? The only thing I do know and am glad I do is that I don't know much of anything. On her bookshelf: volumes of Hokusai, Piranesi, Otto Wagner

2.

From capital to province, and from province to capital, capital was moved provincially. The city on the edge of the volcano, the minaret in the microscope. In my search for the Northwest Passage — I did not discover the Hudson, I invented it. And then reinvented it —

3.

According to the book he was reading by the side of the hotel pool, the first known writing was lists: how much grain was delivered to the palace, how many heads of cattle were received on this or that holy day. Glow-in-the-dark globes in a darkened palazzo —

4.

One loved; one did not love; goods changed hands. She was looking for the seed pearl dropped off the scale in the middle of the vast outdoor market. At the airport, he reached into his bag for his cyanometer — which of fifty different kinds of blue was this particular sky?

5.

And isn't nowhere, after all, also an elsewhere? On her bookshelf: volumes of Audubon, Albert Bierstadt, Edward Curtis — dead birds of paradise, invented mountains, a disappearing culture he believed he alone would make appear and reappear — oh the sublime.

"Proposition 5: Construction should be decorated. Decoration
should never be purposely constructed"

6.

He was told she was busy in the next room, separating form from content. The dazzling embezzler had gone too far, the puzzled Lipizzaner shied from the proffered sugar. Someone had left the newspaper open to the headline: "Sahara once lush and populated."

7.

Goethe's color theory was on her bookshelf. She had visited his house in Weimar, where each room was painted a different color: yellow, red, orange, pink, and his melancholy blue-green study. It was like a violet in formaldehyde, a fallen starling in an airtight jar —

8.

And to this day you find it hard to believe that there are countries in which people eat fruit you've never seen. Behold the blood arriving blue back at the heart after its grand tour of the body. A plaster Taj Mahal atop the bureau, reflected in the mirror expanding behind —

9.

At the origin of every thing is commerce. One loved; one did not love; goods changed hands. Even at the origin of love. With its little store-bought wings. At the airport, the stars finally arrived: the pilot and his flight attendants — unspeakably glamorous.

Inlay 13 (Thomas Mann)

1.

He opened the plain brown book and found inside it a child's stamp collection — tiers of blue butterflies from Equatorial Guinea, rows of cocoa horses from Poland. Who, he wondered, had arranged them in their rows on black pages, a miniature museum appealing straight to the magnifying glass in the mind's eye?

2.

The beautiful lotus-eater in her more industrious schoolgirl days wore coke-bottle glasses. The secret admirer saw it in a photograph kept in a box. Then later, a red hibiscus in her hair. The secret admirer loved to see the husks out of which the hothouse flower grew (as he loved the hothouse flower too).

3.

She was dreamless as a television. And if one day the world map in the atlas matched up with the world map in our mind, we might finally be able to grow fond of it. We might like its lilacs. We might not mind that it always insists Albania lies to the west of Serbia, when we know perfectly well that it lies to the east.

4.

In February came the vacation ads. Figures plunged into blue seas on television screens all over the city. Standing outside the apartment block, she saw all the windows flash and pop at the same time. Somewhere *do* lie the meccas in which our love finds its proportion — somewhere the ziggurat in which the giant inside us snugly fits.

5.

They sat on transatlantiques sipping mugs of hot chocolate, matching up the snow-covered mountains diagrammed on the paper placemat to the snow-covered mountains undiagrammed on the horizon. They were grateful for all the explorers who'd come before them — especially those who'd plunged to their snowy deaths.

"At least he had a sense of order, and even
foolish order is always better than none at all"

6.

Was it the beautiful lotus-eater who'd collected the blue butterfly stamps and placed them where they belonged in the book? If only all objects had their so-obvious slots, and gave such trivial pleasure once they were in them. (The one time a real butterfly flew into her room, she said, she ran, freaked out, out of the house.)

7.

. . . Dreamless as a television. Incorporeal as a television. February. February. February: we kept staring at the statue of the long-forgotten national hero disfigured — revealed — disfigured — revealed — by snow. What was there to do but fuck? It was time for a land grab, or a month's mind, or a velvet cake. It was time for lorgnettes.

8.

Later, winding gingerly through the snowy landscape, they saw airplanes crossing the pale blue sky but couldn't hear them. They heard birds singing in the dark green larch trees but couldn't see them. The helicopter had reduced the once-heroic Saint Bernard to the purgatory of lovable pet, but the brandy still enjoyed savior status.

9.

The secret admirer was snooping; but what else is a secret admirer to do? The secret admirer is after the secret size of his secret object; as the butterfly collector is after the secret joy tangled in the net. The butterfly collector snoops in the forest; the secret admirer snoops in the armoire. Neither gets what it really wants.

Inlay 14 (Walter Benjamin)

1.

He had dedicated every one of his books to his ex-wife, and his new girlfriend opened them one by one: "For Claire." "For Claire." "For Claire." "For Claire." It was spring, that time of the year when the trees outside our windows, briefly, speak, and yet again this year we were unable to understand them.

2.

Blossom, vigil, crane, leaf, steeple. The city was renovating itself building by building. The few unrenovated buildings left among the renovated stood out like outsiders, though they were the real insiders. As for the church: there was money enough in the coffers to renovate its exterior, but not its interior.

3.

This petite eighteenth-century church holding its own among high-rises exuded an exhausted glow. Does "belief" leave any signs behind when the parishioners have filed out; do the notes of the songs just disintegrate or pile up in some secret chalice? The pigeons heavy in the rafters will definitely get to heaven.

4.

Oh yes, she liked the opera, she said, sure — but only the arias. What would life be like, we wondered under the Prussian-blue dome adorned with stars, with only the best parts left in — aria after aria after aria? In 1874, the book said, a Danish mathematician proved that not all infinities are of equal size.

5.

The relics are safe in their gold reliquaries. The roses in the botanical drawings aren't going anywhere, exposed and in the throes of cross-section like beauty submitting to the torture it does call forth of its own accord. Nor is the bee going to get very far, dead on the edge of the windowsill like a spent hedonist.

6.

Another building renovated means another building destroyed. The past is to existence as a garden is to nature: a human construction cruelly dependent on the attentions of the tenders. We saw the scaffolding go up with a sinking feeling. The lush graveyard was flush with blackbirds singing sweetly as the dusk deepened.

"What prevents our delight in the beautiful from ever
being satisfied is the image of the past"

7.

The chair looks solid but it is liquid. From the top of the TV tower, the illusion is complete — the apartment buildings, the churches, the train stations could be trampled as easily as a monster tramples a tiny Tokyo — and so in fact (said the ant), the perspective is no illusion, but reveals a terrible delusion.

8.

The city-that-was was peacefully renovating itself out of existence. Like pieces of a puzzle, a new city was, piece by piece, taking its place. As history after history disappeared, the citizens felt new life behind the scaffolding, behind their own ribcages. The creamy façades captured and gave back the light.

9.

Blossom, lamppost, time, copestone, scaffolding. Who will remember it in the future, the city-that-was? For the photographs are printed in picture books that are made of paper that is produced from trees that are felled in forests that a girl holds like an image of the density of memory in her heart of hearts.

10.

In the distance we could see scaffolding encasing all but the top of a verdigris steeple, like a geometric fur coat. The scaffolding climbed like tin vines up the sides of buildings overnight. We had heard of owls embedded deep in the forests, their yellow eyes embedded deep in their dark feathery heads.

11.

But it was a plastic owl affixed to the top of the roof that shooed off the romantic swallows in us. In the garden we thought we could light our way with the magnolias, but we found out translucency cannot give, it can only receive. On the day the city at last catches up with its history, the city will vanish.

12.

To the blackbirds, the graveyard is just another park. And isn't it? The apartment buildings, the houses, the gravesites, the crosses — the right angle is the principle against which all our circularity rests. "For Claire." "For Claire." "For Claire." "For Claire." The girlfriend put the books back on the shelf.

Inlay 15 (Plato, from Aristotle, from Elaine Scarry)

1.

The disciple asked the prophet of the postmodern: um, whose displacement exactly did you say you were speaking to? Displacement, embankment: some words have liquid centers, like some chocolates. Each day around the world, more and more villagers leave home to disappear into cities.

2.

His secret was safe. Nobody knew how he would sit in the dark of his apartment at night mourning the decline of nation-states. The city glimmered through his curtainless windows, telegraphing its vertical promises and its hollow cores. At the top of the far-off hill, was it a cross or a radio tower?

3.

No one likes walking down a broken escalator. She was wandering through an overgrown orchard on the outskirts of the city when a tree ornate with apples triggered her old desire to be a girl in a Hardy novel: in which a single, starred night of maying would supply the stuff of romance for a lifetime.

4.

I don't know what to say about serial monogamy. I don't know what to say about Chinese chinoiserie. I don't know what to say about the infestation of white butterflies. And I don't know what to say about the dream in which you are chased by a giant Persian kitten through a diorama of Queens.

"Yet, says Plato, it must be the case that the mind is a circle"

5.

Detroit is shrinking. Manchester is shrinking. Leipzig is shrinking. In the souvenir shop she found miniatures of the city in snowglobes. Why is this how one likes to imagine the visited city, forever in the throes of winter? Why is this how one likes to imagine the visited city, fitting into the palm of one's hand?

6.

Walking back to his office the graphic designer stooped to pocket a chestnut. Later, at his desk on the thirty-ninth floor, he felt the speechlessness of the tree work through his head like a benevolent sap. From that day on he secretly carried a chestnut, or a feather, or a small pinecone in his pocket at all times.

7.

It is hard to keep the balance between strangers and acquaintances. Not for the first time, I envied my friend from a small country, where the capital ritually skims the cream from the provinces, and where the obscure language functions like a secret code to keep people from bigger countries in the dark.

8.

I don't know what to say about *épater*ing *les bourgeois*. I don't know what to say about the magnolias in space. I don't know what to say about the reintroduction of foxes. And I don't know what to say about the cosmopolitan obsessively photographing the skyscraper through a replica pinhole camera.

9.

Spiraled seashells from vacation beaches line the windowsills of the landlocked, while sea-green soda bottles wash up in ever greater numbers on the shore; abandoned buildings are blown to pieces in the shrinking cities, while makeshift shacks amass the land in all the cities that expand and expand —

10.

"A white butterfly concerned itself with this lilypad and that catkin. She saw that everything was felt equally by the sunlight — the pond, the maple, the dragonfly, the park bench, the group crossing the footbridge in the distance dressed in white — everything was lovable, from a distance, under the sun"

11.

Schönhauser Allee means Alley of Beautiful Houses. Bellevue means Beautiful View. Bellevue Vista means Beautiful View View. The visitors carried home little refractory cities tamed in glass. It's what every visitor deserves: a beautiful view from a beautiful house among beautiful houses. A beautiful home.

Inlay 16 (Thomas Bernhard)

1.

He wanted to be a citizen of the world and was crushed to discover that the world fields no citizens as such. So he settled for drifting with the voluptés of the clouds. And that is how he met her on a ship from Spain to Morocco, eating clementines and throwing the perfectly spiraled peels into the sea.

2.

Anything is justified as soon as it is doubled. The woman looked distractedly into the cheval glass at her two eyes, two ears, two nostrils, two hands, two legs, and one red-lipsticked mouth. The mirror, one, made two, she and her doppelgänger, who insisted she was she herself, in half a dream.

3.

I loved a man who'd always wanted to be the proprietor of a restaurant. I loved a man who'd always wanted to be the proprietor of a hotel. They were not the same man, she said. But sometimes when I opened my mouth to one, the name of the other would come trotting out like a faithful little dog.

4.

It was true: you had to take an elevator to the top of the ugly building to get a good view of all of the beautiful ones. Even better was to move into the ugly building and spend all day gazing down upon all of the beautiful ones. It is better to receive beauty than to give it — the beautiful would agree.

"Why do painters paint at all, when there is such a thing
as nature? Reger asked himself yesterday, not for the first time"

5.

When hindsight kicked in, she suddenly found herself wearing a diamond choker. It illuminated the world. This too was a kind of doubling: the real occurrence twinned to the occurrence seen cleanly, bereft of its costumes and masks. The occurrence seen by an observer whose motives are pure.

6.

Wie ist dein Name? Pattes, pattes de mouche, thought the citizen of the world smoking an enormous joint in a tiny hotel in the mountains of Morocco. In his view of things, nothing on earth was doubleable. Each star-flower, each roof, each crag in each mountain was relentlessly, ecstatically unique.

7.

No, the occurrence would never recur, that was for sure, except in each glittering square of the disco ball rotating endlessly in her darkened skull. In the bathtub she made the mistake of looking down, for reflected back up at her from the foam was a galaxy of microscopic copies of her guilty hand.

8.

With enough hindsight, couldn't forethought prevent aftereffects? The photographs of the people with their ectoplasms revealed hadn't been convincing *at all*, as anyone with a passing acquaintance with cotton could attest. Why wish to falsify the soul so anyway — why go to such lengths to fool fools?

Inlay 17 (John Ruskin)

1.

It was at an exhibition of clouds, no, at an exhibition of pictures of clouds, all floating in their frames like trapped thoughts. And you wanted to float away on one of them like a ring on a pillow, out of the frame, out of the museum, out of the sky even, no, back down into the sky, to lock the cloud back into place where it belonged in the sky.

2.

The arch was not Gothic but arch-Gothic. The woman with magnolia skin had a drawer in her desk stuffed with little hotel soaps. That night at the Swan Bar, we ordered White Russians, and as we sipped we imagined Russian swans afloat on the half-frozen Neva, floating past a white building we imagined to be made entirely of ice.

3.

The Austrian who was an Anglophile. The Persian who was a Germanophile. The Serbian who was a Sinophile. The American who was a Hellenophile. The Frenchman who was a Francophile. We heard rumors the word "beautiful" was still used in science books, but we never got around to verifying this amazing statement for ourselves.

4.

What is less picturesque than a cloud? Maybe a thought. Maybe a thought about a cloud. Or a thought about a thought clouding over. Or a cloud of thought lost in thought. But clouds *are* thoughts, thought the cloud . . . she thought on the last floor of the exhibition of cloud-pictures, where intolerable transformation was arrested by a pencil.

5.

That winter we never did ice-skate on anything real. Around and around we went on artificial ponds, around and around on our little artificial legs. In the breaths you puffed out into the air I saw genies, vanishing of course as soon as we had formulated our three wishes, each one of which was somehow wasteful and wrong.

"For it might be at first thought that the whole kingdom of imagination
was one of deception also"

6.

The cigar stores stood ready, but where were the nouveaux riches? It was just like ornamental shutters that were never intended to be of any use. And falsified marble streaking its faux violet across the irregular flutes. The Moroccan man collected books about Rome. The Norwegian man had a passion for movies set in Brazil.

7.

Why even try to depict a thing as changeable as a cloud? O intolerable transformation. The catalogue claimed that it was artists who had discovered — or invented — the sky. An impression kept in a snuff bottle. An atmosphere worked in stone. The sky *is* a mind. In which the sugarloafs lurk like the accumulated sediment of thoughts.

8.

That winter he was constantly in the library, hunched over architectural drawings that demonstrated how to convert a Gothic into a Renaissance façade. She stood among the history books, consoled that *something*, even if it *was* the worst of it, would for a while at least remain. What was going to get the snow angels — but snow itself?

9.

In the kingdom of imagination, the train wound its way through the snowy city, disappearing first behind the cathedral and then behind the high-rise, reappearing suddenly all lit up with a mean gold insistence on the horizon. The girl pasted magazine pictures of India, Finland, and Japan in the notebook she kept on her nightstand.

10.

That night she kept dreaming that she was a cloud, perpetually spiraling into another and then another cloud. Perception is a divine matter, make no mistake. And depiction? She thought of the museum as she looked out the window at the clouds. But by the time he got there that evening, the exhibition of cloud-pictures had been taken down.

Inlay 18 (Sei Shonagon)

1.

The city was full of public clocks on poles, but most of them had stopped. One noticed this especially at night. So time itself was a dissembler, just as the city was a dissembler, with all its façades of vivacity belying the lonely contemplation going on under untold circles of lamplight.

2.

The leaves had been on the trees for a long time. Watching the brown squirrel climb around the tree in the park he thought, I like that squirrel more than I like a lot of the people I know. The park was divided into trees, roses, and canals, with only the occasional spiderweb uniting them.

3.

After a life spent gazing with longing at architectural models, one night she began to dream in miniature foyers, with miniature staircases winding up to miniature observatories, all igloo-white. Soon everything that happened in her dreams was tiny, speculative, cold, and sparkling clean.

4.

The pianist had trembling fingers. On the balcony, the flustered girl in the blue crepe de Chine gown lifted a lorgnette to both hide and sharpen her eyes. The state opera house was burned down. And then it was rebuilt. And then again it was burned down. And then again it was rebuilt.

5.

Though we lived in our pigeonholes in postwar apartment blocks, our thoughts were as turreted as châteaux. We kept trying to disentangle beauty from the bourgeoisie, but secretly we knew we *were* the bourgeoisie. As for the shy and the haughty, were *they* really, after all, one and the same?

"I enjoy the way everyone laughs when this happens"

6.

The pond is as still as glass because it is glass, *but we knew that.* There is glass that reveals and glass that conceals, *but we knew that.* The birds don't know the glass skyscrapers are not made of sky, *but we knew that.* The glass in the window liquefies because it is liquid *but we knew that.*

7.

A leaf fell off a tree across the platform and then rose up into the sky — it wasn't a leaf, but a leaflike butterfly. She had always avoided the butterfly exhibit at the zoo, reasoning that beauty should never be massed. His upward mobility sat hidden, in wait, plotting and clawing with hopes.

8.

Let's build our utopian society in the abandoned houses of Detroit. Of necessity is a fountain, to drown out all the blathering of the world. If we all only said what was necessary, couldn't we hear the ant bearing its crumb of chocolate cake out of the kitchen, out of the house, into oblivion?

9.

The shy are misperceived as the haughty, but the haughty are never shy. Out of the cuckoo clock came not a cuckoo, but a tiny speaker broadcasting the call of the muezzin. We didn't know who the joke was on, but what *was* certain was that we would be among the laughing.

Inlay 19 (Jane Jacobs)

1.

And then it was the first of August. The remainder of the summer suddenly seemed so fragile that we willed its demise even while watching apprehensively as day declined into day declined into day. Even the leaves on the trees seemed ransomed. The summer was nothing but a stage set, but we performed our summer roles.

2.

Standing in front of the new building, we wondered what the architect could *possibly* have been thinking. We didn't mind that we were reactionaries who wanted Palladio back on the pedestal. A column, a portico, a finial, a turret, an oriel, an ogival arch. O in Venice we were ecstatic with ogives, ogives, ogives.

3.

The story is always forming to adorn reality. Which version is more magnetic, more true? The ivory-billed woodpecker glimpsed in the bayou, or the dinosaur skeleton discovered in the heart of the desert by a French countess dressed as a man? They said it was just beyond the next dune, after the third oasis, the fourth mirage.

4.

In the cabinet of wonders dismantled into the glass case there were ivory miniatures: saints, castles, madonnas, migrations — carved by a patience it is impossible even for the elephant to remember. "We" are no longer tantalized by the tiny. And what *of* the entire book of Exodus carved into a single cherry pit?

5.

An oasis may or may not be a mirage, said the camel on its knees in the dark caravansaray. Oh the oasis was real, all right, but when we left it we could not have said if the mirage had been in us or if we had been in the mirage. There is a viewfinder through which everything is seen — mirages, *and* oases, *and* —

6.

Every mind has a curiosity cabinet, in which curious objects "intended for private reflection" mount up to protect it against an incurious world. The spectacled cormorant sits in its engraving, in its frame, in its museum, in its country it never heard tell of. A ship must have its naturalist. A zoo must have its metaphysician.

7.

The architects, we said, have failed us, and turned slowly away. We ate pink petits-fours. It was less painful to be in the new cities, which had never known the beauty they would now never have, than the old cities, desperate to be new. In the new city we undressed each other with great care, as if we were unwrapping fragile glass.

“the necessary transactions of decline”

8.

Every mind has its own curiosity cabinet, which is why everyone is, at bottom, an aristocrat. She knew that she was imprisoned in a garden of giant man-eating nostalgia flowers as she reminisced, and reminisced, and reminisced. Nostalgia is memory decayed to sugar, she thought on a bench in the plaza of a massive glass box.

9.

Two sisters from a small American town both confessed to an attraction for the exotic. But for one the exotic meant India, and for the other it meant Japan. Why? A story is always forming to adorn reality. The last passenger pigeon opened its long, slim tail and flew up, high, high into the bright white clouds of extinction.

10.

Childhood is miniature. Memory is miniature. The stars are, after all, miniature. The summer was not miniature, is never miniature, the summer among the towers, among the cloverleaf highways. The first day of August was followed by the first night of August. You fed me pink petits-fours and I dreamed of destruction.

II.

An oasis may or may not be a mirage, but a mirage is always an oasis. The room I'm reading in is only one of legions in the speculative castle. This domain is eminent. The architects have failed us, but aren't we all, somehow, in the end, to blame? By the time we applied our eye to the viewfinder, the great auk was gone.

Inlay 20 (Franz Kafka)

1.

Would you fold yourself up into a suitcase to cross a wall? and other vanity questions making the rounds of the parlor. A monster passed me in the park. The clouds were so high up in the clouds were so high up in the clouds

"What could have enticed me to this desolate country

2.

She said, "I saw a glimmer of cruelty in his beautiful blue eyes and that's when I knew I could love him." Would you dig a tunnel, secretly, at night, for three years? An altar made of salt. A chapel, a cathedral, a Vatican made of salt.

3.

In China, mothers buy their children crickets in cages. The rain falling on the pond revealed the pond's inner geometrist, describing perfect circles as if to the manor born. Which maintained perfection as they widened out into nothing.

4.

Would you let your girlfriend sew you a facsimile of a Russian greatcoat, then show up at the checkpoint as "Igor," saying *"Propustite menya"?* The clipping slowly ivories in its album. The belletristic druggist was secretly studying theosophy.

5.

It was hard to tell the reflection of the underbrush from the voluminous moss vitiating the pond from within. It was hard to believe formlessness could be perfectly circular. The angel at the top of the victory column smiled fixedly at the defeated country.

6.

Would you ride in the engine compartment of a vw folded into a pretzel for nine hours? The host demonstrated, to the great merriment of the mildly soused guests. The old cosmopolitan in the corner sat thoughtfully stroking a snow white cat.

7.

In a blitzkrieg of a stranger's perfume I was suddenly illuminated. I tore myself away from the pond and its lessons about surface and depth: 1) That surface can *have* depth. 2) That depth wants to be devoured by surface. I walked on violets.

8.

In China mothers buy their children crickets in cages, but if the cricketing gets on her nerves, the little holy man gets destroyed. Nobody can say for sure how long the euphoria lasts on the other side, or how long it takes to unfold out of the trunk.

except the wish to stay here?"

9.

Would you rip your hands to shreds on barbed wire? Jump from the ninth story? Punishable by death. And other curiosities I saw in a book. The party guests all went home with their heads radiating their own desires, which widened out into nothing.

Inlay 21 (Ralph Waldo Emerson)

1.

Of the seven wonders of the ancient world, only one is still in existence today. I wanted you to be my Louisiana Purchase, my Alaska. But when we walked past the Titanic travel bureau, even a night drowning in our dreamworld promised more salt than a scene of real happiness from our past locked in ice.

2.

The longer and farther we were apart, the more I thought our letters could sew our velvet minds together. Do not linger long on the Persian carpet — that is the only advice I have left in my echoing vial. It was as if someone had said "Macbeth" in a theater — so many houses of cards collapsed through the trap door.

3.

The American man who was living in Tanzania was an expatriate, but the Tanzanian man who was living in North America was an immigrant. Every year just before Christmastime, a pale starburst lamp is hung from a hook on the darkened evangelical church, glowing like an amulet at the throat of a ghost.

4.

Of the seven wonders of the *modern* world, there has been little consensus. When he told her he was "travelling the world collecting material for future nostalgias," she thought of the narrow hallway she had once walked along hung entirely with mirrors — rectangular, circular, oval, oblong, and convex.

5.

Wieland was called "the German Voltaire," but Voltaire was never called "the French Wieland." Have you been to the Paris of the East. We had packed some bottles of beer and a volume of poems and set off in quest of the ideal landscape, which was not to be found in any country we called our own.

> ". . . and yet how evanescent and superficial is most of that emotion which names & places, which Art or magnificence can awaken . . ."

6.

The young border policeman paged through her passport greedily and yet delicately: like a kitten she had seen with a baby bird in its black paws. You were shown the whole of my Wunderkammer, my worked coral, my mandrake root, my glass beads I tried to trade for gold. The Baltic Sea is overfished.

7.

Of the seven wonders of the ancient world, you said you had only ever wondered at one. And at that moment, passing through the blue Ishtar Gate, in a museum, in a city, in a country, on a continent, on a planet —. Over a double espresso he said, “I hate the phrase ‘late capitalism.’ Maybe it’s actually very early.”

8.

Coming out of the design studio they realized that everything they saw, every kiosk, every park bench, every streetlamp, was the end result of a process of narrowing down thousands upon thousands of choices. Only the brown birds flitting through the pollarded trees seemed free of the funnel of the human mind.

9.

I thought of the silence between us as snow, cold but gentle, protecting the impulses of spring till the time of spring. But a letter was sent to me from a country I had never heard of, covered in stamps of the most beautiful ice-blue — and then the port appeared, a cove carved into a glacier, a white place to moor.

Inlay 22 (Elfriede Jelinek, by way of Lenin)

1.

In Cologne we bought cologne. In Morocco we bought morocco. In Kashmir we bought cashmere. Then, our suitcases stuffed, we flew back home to New York City, where we drank manhattan after manhattan until ill-advisedly late into the evening.

2.

"I'm an anarchist," said the poet. "You're spoiled," said his girlfriend. A line of people in masks paraded by. And then the lights dimmed, and the one true anarchist was suddenly spotlit in the crowd: a little girl with an ice cream sandwich melting in her bag.

3.

The beautiful people wanted to go only to places where there were other beautiful people, in cafés and restaurants and bars, and puffed nervously on their cigarettes when the number of ugly people shown to tables seemed to be reaching critical mass.

4.

You like to be told what to do. You like to be shown to your plug and to glow in it like a nightlight. You like to be clued in, strapped on, knuckled under. You like to be held down and liquored up. You like to be scooped out, bowled over, seen through.

"Trust is fine, but control is better"

5.

Forking over our dollars, we hatched a grand plan for the overlapping economy: Let the French take care of the perfumes; the Dutch of the tulips; and the Italians of the leather shoes. Each would be a department in the department store in the Great Mall.

6.

She wrote, I want to be seen through. He wrote, But you are deliberately opaque. She wrote, I want people to want to work hard to see through my (really quite superficial) opacity. He wrote nothing back. She waited, but he wrote nothing back.

7.

You like to go from room to room drowning yourself in dahlias. You like to stand in a crowd and implode and implode till all your individuality melts. You like to be underneath, on top, afloat. But it thrills you to hear your name in a stranger's mouth.

8.

Was it good or bad when the foreigner was said to be "more French than the French"? She of the huge hats and humble origins was "more bourgeois than the bourgeois." And the cosmopolitan was more cosmopolitan than the cosmos itself.

9.

We bought china in China. We bought cognac in Cognac. You bought turquoise in Turkey, and I bought an afghan in Afghanistan. I bought india ink in India, and you bought an indiaman in India. But nowhere did we relinquish any little bit of ourselves.

Sources of Inlays

Inlay 1: Franz Kafka: *The Trial*

Inlay 2: Elaine Scarry: *Dreaming by the Book*

Inlay 3: Jonathan Raban: *Coasting*

Inlay 4: Susan Sontag: *Regarding the Pain of Others*

Inlay 5: Erwin Panofsky: *Meaning in the Visual Arts*

Inlay 6: Mary B. Campbell: *The Witness and the Other World*

Inlay 7: Franz Kafka: *The Trial*

Inlay 8: Claude Lévi-Strauss: *Tristes Tropiques*

Inlay 9: Azar Nafisi: *Reading Lolita in Tehran*

Inlay 10: Ralph Waldo Emerson: Apocryphal

Inlay 11: Zaha Hadid: Interview on NPR

Inlay 12: Owen Jones: *The Grammar of Ornament*

Inlay 13: Thomas Mann: *Doctor Faustus*

Inlay 14: Walter Benjamin: "On Some Motifs in Baudelaire"

Inlay 15: Plato, Aristotle, Elaine Scarry: *Dreaming by the Book*

Inlay 16: Thomas Bernhard: *Old Masters*

Inlay 17: John Ruskin: *The Seven Lamps of Architecture*

Inlay 18: Sei Shonagon: *The Pillow Book of Sei Shonagon*

Inlay 19: Jane Jacobs: *Cities and the Wealth of Nations*

Inlay 20: Franz Kafka: *The Castle*

Inlay 21: Ralph Waldo Emerson: *Letters*

Inlay 22: Elfriede Jelinek, by way of Lenin: *The Piano Teacher*

Colophon

The Cosmopolitan was designed at Coffee House Press,
in the historic warehouse district of downtown Minneapolis.
The type is set in Garamond.

Funders

Coffee House Press is an independent nonprofit literary publisher. Our books are made possible through the generous support of grants and gifts from many foundations, corporate giving programs, state and federal support, and through donations from individuals who believe in the transformational power of literature. This book received special support from the National Poetry Series. Coffee House Press receives general operating support from the Minnesota State Arts Board, through an appropriation by the Minnesota State Legislature and from the National Endowment for the Arts, and major general operating support from the McKnight Foundation, and from Target. Coffee House also receives support from: two anonymous donors; the Elmer L. and Eleanor J. Andersen Foundation; Bill Berkson; the Buuck Family Foundation; the Patrick and Aimee Butler Family Foundation; Jennifer Haugh; Joanne Hilton; Stephen and Isabel Keating; the Kenneth Koch Literary Estate; Allan and Cinda Kornblum; Seymour Kornblum and Gerry Lauter; Kathryn and Dean Koutsky; Ethan J. Litman; Mary McDermid; Stu Wilson and Melissa Barker; the Lenfestey Family Foundation; Rebecca Rand; the law firm of Schwegman, Lundberg, Woessner, P.A.; Charles Steffey and Suzannah Martin; the James R. Thorpe Foundation; the Woessner Freeman Family Foundation; the Wood-Rill Foundation; and many other generous individual donors.

This activity is made possible in part by a grant from the Minnesota State Arts Board, through an appropriation by the Minnesota State Legislature and a grant from the National Endowment for the Arts.

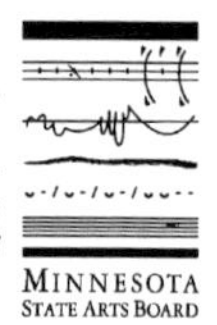

To you and our many readers across the country,
we send our thanks for your continuing support.

Good books are brewing at coffeehousepress.org